Beauty Breaks In

Mary Ann Samyn

New Issues Poetry & Prose

A Green Rose Book

New Issues Poetry & Prose
The College of Arts and Sciences
Western Michigan University
Kalamazoo, Michigan 49008

Inland Seas poetry books are supported by a grant from
The Michigan Council for Arts and Cultural Affairs

Printed in the United States of America.

First Edition, 2009.

ISBN-10 1-930974-87-6 (paperbound)
ISBN-13 978-1-930974-87-6 (paperbound)

Library of Congress Cataloging-in-Publication Data:
Samyn, Mary Ann
Beauty Breaks In/Mary Ann Samyn
Library of Congress Control Number: 2009924364

Art Direction: Tricia Hennessy
Design: Locklin McKinnon
Production: Paul Sizer
The Design Center, Frostic School of Art
College of Fine Arts
Western Michigan University

Beauty Breaks In

Mary Ann Samyn

New Issues

Western Michigan University

Beauty Breaks In

Also by Mary Ann Samyn

Rooms by the Sea
Captivity Narrative
Inside the Yellow Dress
Purr

Contents

I can't see it, I can't see it, and then—

—Ann Hamilton

It is a leap of faith to put this in an open space, but I take a chance.

—Louise Bourgeois

Lift the forest floor, slightly.

—Jo McDougall

A Girl Can Imagine, Can't She, a Girl Can Dream

Now then. This won't hurt a bit. Boys & Girls. Yes, I promise. Verbs explain how to do it.

This page is full of words in much the same way I can't sleep some nights between two and four.

If you think you know, then you probably don't, thank goodness, or we couldn't be friends.

He developed special instruments to probe and extract the bullet, after which he applied a styptic . . .

For information about this account, press 1; for a little push ("Go away." "Submit."), hold the line.

Look at yourself in the mirror. Pin the parts together to look like a body. Make your final pattern.

Eyes far apart mean younger; eyes close together mean shrewder; children need only a small stitch.

O Sister Miriam of the Holy Spirit, O Sister Rose of God, am I not His Little Question-Mark?

Lively does it, fish line or strong linen thread, a large-eyed needle, and you measure and you measure.

The wonder of it is how and why if you really want to have fun with electricity as famously illustrated.

Some dolls walk and talk. I knew one who blew bubbles. One with stiff limbs and a soft cloth body.

I practice being serious. I practice love of knowledge. I practice busyness. I practice the braver way.

O honeybee, what sweet results are wrought by industry. If you doubt that I am happy, listen to me hum!

In the background, velvet. A small table for my stage. Flood lights, silence, your attentive gaze.

The hand here depicted contains a great deal of information. I don't sit still and hope and wonder.

The cupboard as it should look. Nouns in a row. I'm just as surprised as you are. Action = Reaction.

Try these activities. Don't worry. Follow directions and diagrams. You will have a great deal of fun.

Some dolls tear up. Also, the Virgin Mary. The pull of a string. A garden or alcove. *Oh my.*

So daily I aimed for something practical, something personal, something charitable, something spiritual.

Consider *Ben and the Green Corduroy Angel.* Consider this a little page of no thanks to you.

Electricity doesn't just happen. Oh no? This story was not made up. My town stood still for eight hours.

"Your whole life would be different if you had a chart with feet on it." Well, I guess that's right.

For assessment purposes, please list three visions worth working toward and three dumb questions.

The first step in the writing process is "romancing." The third is "writing." The last is "showing off."

Some dolls prefer a more pragmatic, reality-oriented practice. Some surgeons admire their own work.

Who will read my work and what is special about my writing that will make my readers glad?

If you are experiencing an emergency, by all means, proceed to your local emergency room.

If you would like to make up jump-rope rhymes using the multiplication facts, please go elsewhere.

O Sister Miriam, O Sister Rose, *how great the lions and tigers are, filling the air with sound!*

Arrows mean movement. Numbers mean help is on the way. When you press the button, it lights up.

Imagine this poem sequenced movie-style. Frame by frame by frame. Which scenes are you missing?

Make a list of eight ways to cook without electricity, nine ways to tell time, a dozen uses for eggshells.

He was dexterous. She was lovely. He was brusque. She was fervent. He was gentle. She was stormy.

Gather together, give entertainments, illustrate interesting points in history, practice, practice, practice.

Sometimes a question mark is also used inside parentheses after a date or statement to show doubt.

The answer is transfigure. List as many questions as you can think of for which that is the answer.

6

7

An Ambiguity

—Watched myself go toward effortlessness: smart move à la beech and hemlock.

As for the thoughtless remark, I couldn't keep my field straight from my ground, couldn't keep my mouth shut after.

As far as metaphors go, I'm working with forest succession at the moment: "silent testimony"/"sun-loving pioneer": catch my drift?

Ave Maria polishes the background, while I tidy up out front.

Want to enjoy some majesty? Come on by, rain or snow, any evening.

Bank on It

No, wait— I told the story.

Then, start it, by God.

(Hello?) (Cashier?)

I shimmied up.

I'm in this pattern now.

Put my forms in the slot.

Dinner almost every night.

What more do you want.

Whatever you resist, persists,
said everyone famously.

Buzz Buzz Buzz

I hate when people are irrational someone irrational once said.
I cut up the small Bible and called it *Deliver me to my beauty.*
And it did.

Here's what I have in mind:
the cabin lights are dimmed,
between my shoulder and yours, a forever-and-ever sound.

Cautionary

Peeling back the *oh look!*, there's more.

—Set that aside.
And set that aside.
And set that aside.

. . . and if, when on your Lenten Journey, you need a friend . . .

CRASH-BANG!

I learned a long time ago;

cue the ocean; all my small-time hopes wait on a big gesture;

it's a crawlspace, right?

And read again from *The Mystery at Lilac Inn*:

> "Nancy's fear gave way to curiosity . . ."

—the *therein* contained therein.

Churned Up

The wind got a little nervy.

Some April—, I heard myself say.

So much for happiness without trying.

Consider this one more volume of progress, unabridged.

Or not. Like so much else, it's up to you.

I lied when I said I enjoyed not knowing for certain.

For certain is my dearest friend.

Nonetheless, this is an expansionist moment.

Fortunately, I am spectacularly adept.

Cinder Box

Soot on our streets for traction and
at the corners of our mouths.

Same purpose, same result.
Dismay, dismay.

But I keep at it. *Real trooper.*
Boot through it.

Something sneaky goes on, dimly,
I'm aware.

But the solution is equally murky,
sluggish as our new river.

Which way the train whistle goes,
I sometimes wonder.

The interruption is brief,
like mercy,

concealed as I am: a hood of *quieter*,
a hood of consent.

Clarity, 1.2

—Considering The Despair of St. Thomas.

(Tame it.)

—Considering *Lion and Cage*: wire, yarn, etc.

If you don't know a word, you should look it up:
translucence is one thing; transparency, further down.

How much do you shine through?

(why O why)

This is my face: frequently human.

This is the line for joy.

Content / Content

In the hollow, the hollow was everything.
We oohed and aahed appropriately.
We learned sandstone versus limestone versus
what might have been.

There's happiness and then
there's resignation. *Fine.*
Diamonds. *Fine.* Dust.

What we liked best was anticipation,
which was fortunate since that was what we got.

And over every word you said, a pebble.
And over every word I said, a pebble kicked.

Yes, I stole this idea from art,
which precedes articulation which precedes science
and *all the rage.*

Can you blame me?

For $9 we got the one hour tour. For a little more,
could have had a hard hat and crawlspace,
could have had total loss.

Thanks, but no, we said. Meaning: been there,
grappled with that.

I like my emptiness with a bit of elbow room.
You like yours with a convenient hatch.

Covenant

—Third time's the charm. But so far,
twice this week, this word.

Very Old Testament, *God said* . . . , etc.

Very painful to consider in light of.

I had written down my wish. No,
my prayer. I have it still.

And can you believe it was answered.

Now I must own up regardless of all else.

Now a very red bird or puff of cloud
could distract you.

But a good reader knows better.

I'm here to say the plainest thing.

Don't Ruin It

—Moving from dose to dose:
It's just suffering.

Tease it out.

Technique alone won't work.

You should know that by now. By now
is moveable, of course, *but still—*

I had a professional moment right before
a less professional one.

All right already.

Remember the leaf walks of elementary school Octobers?
Appreciate this, kids.

And I did. Still do. Crunch Crunch Crunch.

Can't argue with that logic.

Everyone's doing it. The trees showed us how. Etc.

The thing is, I've got a crush on progress.
As always.

So there's hope, right? Metaphor Metaphor Metaphor.

I want to talk more about this.
How's tomorrow?

Everything Sounds Almost Right In Poems

Or do I mean poetry? If I had a schedule, I'd expect the train to whistle on cue, which it does though I don't. Took me what felt like all afternoon to tie transparent thread around the neck of a doll-sized aspirin bottle. Next, I'll use a thumbtack to install it in my "Cloud Nine/Sister(')(s)(') Repair Kit." I'm snapping my fingers to make 5:15 happen faster. Then 5: whatever, then whatever: whatever. What I do when I'm not doing this, I can't say. The dolls—brunettes—specialize in smugness. As for reading and being read, they're against it. If I put them on a train, they show up at the next station, right on time. If I write them into a poem as I've been advised, it's like I believe it.

From *The Little Book of Female Mystics*

—Can't you see that I am not the person I was? Time is no more than the point of a needle. Same goes for suffering. Once I said, "always eat your protein first." And mostly I got stronger. Now knowledge grows more intense, and lustrous as a pelt. Not all visionary experiences are created equal; Catherine of Siena and Christ exchanged hearts. The sadness of church is the sadness of what could have been. The sadness of me, ditto. I am not wishing to be an anchoress. I am not counting on anything. I am remembering learning to swim—no metaphor—at the Bambi Motel, Sault Sainte Marie, Michigan. If this is pride, then sometimes I too am amazed my soul stays in my body. Does God monitor such thoughts? I'm thinking not.

Having Come This Far

The loneliness was so old!
I had celebrated all of its birthdays.

Some verbs need helpers, my mother used to say.
Like the strings of an apron at the small of her back.

Today, a bird lay down in the grass.
Just like that, I'm telling myself.

If you knew how I thought of you,
you would say: this is a poem of praise.

Her Sun Was Blue, Her Tree Was Green, Her Line Was Very Straight

Another dazzling finale
and then I get to choose the braver way.

Tomorrow and tomorrow and tomorrow
are the questions.

Be still, be quiet, be calm and watch,
the best advice I know.

If I could wave a magic wand, I would.

Remembering is such a thrill
the rain does it all day long.

This is the current dread.
This, the nest of birds outside our window.

I Darken It Besides

—Then the other part pulled back and the white showed through:

the option.

But where was the *sought out*? The barely red and telling
bit of something female in the hedge . . .

I had prayed like this.

Instead, my shadow against the snowy side of the house.
Wind gone first this way, then that.

<thinking / darting / thinking>

—which was the look I had, adjusting the fit of the new

at the wrists, at the ruffled neck . . .

What I mean to say diminishes bit by bit:

curl of, curl up—

I cup my hands around my mouth for warmth.
I breathe the same air twice.

I Took Myself to Task

It's an ancient feeling: *Hey—*
It's what percentage guilt deferred?
Someday the stakes will have been pulled up.
This is what we call The Merciful Hand of God.
Is this adulthood or just bad fate? Friend, I'm guessing.
Exquisite is a word with a cut. See my hand:
I mean, lip:
Autumn is not quite my favorite scenery.
Today's bluster is clean but welcome.

I Want You to Scream It

I was crouching in the craft aisle. I was taking just a few notes on The Effect of Vodka on the Underlying Sadness.

For heaven's sake, don't worry. It's just Wal-Mart: paintbrushes and paint, some talent and a little *hey why not.*

I could make it snowy midnight, if you want. I could sweep my arms and be your trusted guide.

Watch: I'm doing astonishment here. I'm giving us both permission. *Open 24 hours* was invented by me.

I Whispered *Oh* into His Ear

Lack was the message.

Such is life, I've heard.

I found my God good and ready

—want some?—,

my mercy right where I left it.

This is the first in a series:

Self-portrait as Who Am I to Say?.

Do you like it? Will you buy it?

How much?

I only made a peep to start.

The power is in prediction.

In a Dark Time Together

All day I say every blessings I can think of.
In the evening I study the empty votive jars:
pictures of saints in their private distress.
I touch where their lips just barely open:
whatever it is that entered, entered here.
One jar I stuff with gauze, keeping it quiet.
One with greasy nuts and bolts.
One, the Lonely Soul, with three red darts
to pierce the sooty air.

In the Countryside of *The*

Hey, forgiveness, I said, catching a glimpse.

This was prehistoric in the sense that I had no idea.

This was a picnic in the sense that something might have blown away.

Thank goodness for mythology, which supplied the speaking parts and a reason to lie down.

Thank goodness for tomorrow, which held today, squirming a little but secretly loving it.

Incredibly Small and Impossibly Lovely

Don't fight it, I tell myself, *build a monument instead.*
Why must everything be visible to the naked eye?

There are ghost towns aplenty in my favorite state.
Maybe in another life I lived on their fringes.

Tonight's moon is one way sorrow earns its keep.
Maybe I can patent tomorrow's strong sunrise.

Introducing the Bird-watcher to the Bird

Note: we began in error: a tingling.

*

You queried.

*

But have you a library, a system, an instrument?

*

—I shot back.

*

Thus, what had been null and void:

*

Dear Amateur—

*

Now we flit into view:

*

one calling out, each nightfall, the other

*

(sorry—)

*

begging back.

An Introduction to Devotion

Do you consider yourself adept? The face of

oh my and the body of a wish: this is the error

of sadness. Now you say, *don't implicate me.*

Too late, sweetness. As in the Bonnie & Clyde dream . . .

Relentlessly acquisitive. As in, get ready

for us, God. This is small-time rapture. Soothe me.

Or else, I said to no one in particular. *Back off—!*

It Most Certainly Is Edged in White

The book of birds knew a little about a lot.

I flipped through.

No one said trying harder would be easy.

A dove's identifying feature

may or may not be peacefulness;

disjunction had been a performance;

I stopped complaining.

Starting now, no prayer goes unanswered.

It's Been a Lovely October Thus Far

—Got the gist of it down; had another apple from the snack pack,
pre-sliced for my convenience.

The high school band practice drifts my way.

Will I always be lonely in towns with small-time civic pride?

At least I've done a good job of not filling the nothingness
with more of the same.

I consider the berries on the ivy: each one a little entrance
or exit.

My strength I learned a long time ago.

Loud and Clear

This is the moment you've been waiting for:

this God and what this God wants.

The paperback of *yes* arrives right on schedule.

Alone in a crowd? Indian Summer?

The right answers are contained herein;

I'm more and more myself.

Come on,

a little mayhem goes a long way;

you know

darkness makes for the most vivid sleep.

Make a Musical of It

Fluctuations revved up my skin. Pleasant/
not so. I've been dramatic in my day.
Listen from within said the seashell
to the main girl I was. Put a nimbus
around that: *the kingdom of God*
as I've come to know it, expertly.
Ounces and ounces certainly do add up,
the prop master said, hauling emotion.
Hell, yeah was my fist in the air.

Make Them Howl or Breathe Fire

I was strung up.
I was my own angel.
Repeat: I was my own angel.
Something beeped to signal the end of mercy.
          Oh well—
Weather swirled just beyond my shoulder.
Had I not been on my knees already.
Had I not grasped the concept.
God likes firm resolve.
I detest all my sins. Above all, ingratitude, the color of which pales,
   like my skin.

Nail

There are a myriad of options. Menu-board.

Would you like something fluted or barbed?

Big difference. *Big deal*, I say to myself

to bring it down a notch. A little humility

and a winning smile have been my method.

There's a place for everything and everything

holds this house together. Are you the art project

I am? Are you rigged? The dictionary says

one variant is as good as another. *Oh please—*.

What you might call *fixed*, I call *intent*.

Opting for Natalie Wood Over Poetry

On her left wrist a bracelet, always, hiding an error she knew was there.

I look at the pictures but don't see anything out of the ordinary.

If I had, I'd have to go toward it. I mean this spiritually.

All the while giving thanks for favors not yet received.

That's the new strategy: tilt my head à la Natalie and smile her smile.

Not on account of God so much, but because of mirrors:

if I catch even the slightest look of fear, I choose it.

Part Two: Mystery

Little wonder: first star from my left eye:

casual wink

I'm practicing, my mouth a bit caught up . . .

Behind the scenes: pulleys move what needs a new view.

As usual, mechanics impress.

Once when I was five, and brutal,

my hair a dark note,

my mouth—

Once when the rehearsal split open, I crawled to safety.

Now the implication is

folded just so.

See—?

The edge of it glistens. And your hand,

your hand comes down hard.

Ply Me with Something, Please

—Stirring sounds from inside—
          My husband making *mojitos*,
          the Cuban drink we've just discovered.

Is this a come-on from the kitchen?

You can only make something absorb so much is what I say
          when he appears and the discussion turns to sugar.

What's saturated is saturated.

. . . though science seems far off: the law
          of *prove it to me*.

Out on the porch, one candle flickers a little too intently.

The others are for saints and would burn just fine all night
          if I let them.

I think of Saint Joseph, buried, upside down, for luck
          in the garden of the house we left.

All winter, he wintered.

This is how I remember panic: white, at the edges.

But for now, just this vague happiness:
          my finger along the sweet rim.

Prototype

Put a nipple here to pacify it.

Good. Now,

a command to show who's boss.

If you want the mystical, this is a fine time.

Then, a wand and bubbles, a little hope

you can carry in your purse.

And three yeses, just in case,

and noes I think you've got.

Is this a place you'd like to live?

Sure, there's some anger.

There's a process.

This is the new definition of *peninsular*.

Waves lap the shore.

If you don't believe me, look up.

Quarterly Report

Is wistfulness a sin? I'm wondering.

This too is the day the Lord has made.

Boy oh boy, I sigh, beachcombing.

Found one state fossil for free.

What God hath joined together.

The luck here runs that clear.

Could glaciation work thus on me?

I'm readiness, personified.

I don't begrudge the spider her web.

We've all got work we're doing.

This lapse is momentary, mottled.

What emerges, emerges distinctly.

Riskier Still

The tree book says, choose a shape.

(Intuition flares)

My mother wants to know, am I in town?

Infinite Crisis #5.

I'm temper, underneath.
I'm pacing all the way through.

Sketch it out.

Glossy at the edges.

Wow, you said, *those are sharp*.

Say of Me What You Will

Listen, a girl gets angry.

A girl—   strike that—

Look, what we have here is a girl who fights like a girl.

                (Too bad.)

Also, a cave a girl something something or other.

Come on, everybody now—

                To-morrow, to-morrow*!*

                (sing-songy, old-timey)

                Hello, hello*!*

                (mile for mile)

                (a girl wonderland)

Now there's a sound you'll not hear again.

Standard girl. Kick-the-can girl.

Trademark. Slump-down. Elbows out . . .

. . . *Her eyes close by means of a lever* (the book says so)
that runs through her head and body and comes out—
like a pinch in reverse—*at her hip.*

Sleuth

Panting: the hauled up | thing between us.

We are at the beach. | *Tell yourself.* | I tell myself.

Birds (white with black legs; black head with orange legs; solemn gray)
chatter or wait all in one direction.

"Strange sense of déjà vu," says G.

If I were 12, I'd detect . . .   *amiss.*

Even now, my mind peeks around the hibiscus
to catch what?—small—love?—scoot

—no, just our friend anole, out of sight.

Smack-dab

—So when I passed out of childhood, part of me stayed behind:
    a little wave.

Yet this does not fully explain prayer's necessity and danger. I know;
    trust me.

If you press a cheek to the window of your pulse (are you following?)
    as I do—

If you are very stoic when hurt, like an animal—   Then maybe
    you're getting it.

Little by little is one way to row a boat. Mine is blue and white
    and very very sleepy.

Yours I cannot say. But I'm betting on the unimaginable,
    and the painfully obvious.

Some Churches

My name fits the forms: . . . *you who, pray for us* . . .
My knees, the kneeler.

This arch arches dark;
drawn in sorrow, chalky Christ.

That's ok.
I prefer my mosaics in a messy heap.
Shard. Shard. Shard. Every plea
nearly answered.

Milk it is what I tell myself. The moment of *one moment*
please—I'll connect you. Before the tangled *hello*—.
Before the static *husband*?.

—Only more so
and unrelentingly. Not sure if this is a museum
or if I am. *Room 8: Competing Tendencies.*

I heard the coins hit bottom.
I saw my ticket torn in jagged halves.

Now, a tiny placard begs *Please do not cross this line.*

—toe to toe, here's a chip of wistfulness winking out;
here's my characteristic vacant stare.

Something Must Be Left to the Mystery

Got a Fancy Pony in a cellophane bag.
Hong Kong.
Thought, Fancy Pony could be my guide!
(having just remembered about guides)
Good answer, good answer, I heard myself say,
husky, confident-like.
Game-show-speak
as when families duke it out.
The thing was, a lot of guides had tried and failed:
the Japanese cat with its one paw held high;
the tiny tiny vase I imagined I could crawl inside;
the cube that stumped me again and again;
my husband.
Sparkle sparkle had been my mantra
so long—
Patience, my downfall.
"Why now?" the new book wondered.
Because—, I whinnied,
and stamped my foot against the ground.

Suppose We Make That Assumption

These trees were cut illegally.

Which leaves us what? And why?

I'm reminded of rhythmic gymnastics,
which may or may not be a sport,
which entrances as it perplexes.

I'm reminded that I can do this.

O, long ago, how I keep you with me,
etc. on and on.

I said something to myself to start it,
something less successful to stop.

What did you say to yourself?

If I were a box, I'd have a big red ribbon,
no wanting about it. But, also,
a not-nice ooze along all my edges . . .

This is a problem.

—So how *did* Emily Dickinson bake bread?
That's what I want to know.

How will I recognize you when you arrive?

How will you know me dressed as I am
in rhetoric and light?

Tell 'em Why You're Special

I'm about to remember something right on schedule.

Not: my mother bought three coats, kept the receipt, returned two.

But from that same era.

This is my proof, God. I've got a good mind. I've got a mind to.

Now, whole days pass. I am unaccountably.

Punitive is a word they teach you.

Were there twigs in my hair then, a leftover half-note?

I tucked into it.

So weird! They let me out that way.

So weird, *this, now.*

That's the Jesus I Grew Up With

Lateral, divergent: I'm paying me a compliment.
My God had a heart-shaped heart, and a look.
I never knew what bribe was coming next.
Something was disheveled. Was it my hair
in butterfly barrettes? Was it my grown-up soul?
I led with fear, Mother and Dad; sit down.
Dusk was always the favorite, with its gorgeous regret.

There's No Time Like the Present

Read Rich at the Grease Monkey, Ashbery at the softball game.
Yes, hello, I'm fine. And you?

Thus seven days make one week.

From the plane I admired South Dakota—what lines! what efficiency!

While Charles told it to me straight: "Memory's logo
is the abyss, and that's no metaphor." God!

Right now I'm getting ready to turn my longing into contentment.
Getting ready to be lovely someday, very very lovely.

When the plane sped up, I guess I did too.

My thinking, evolving.

When you're in the right mood, clouds look like animals, etc.
When you're not, they don't.

Often the most beautiful looking books don't help at all.
I think they will, but no such luck.

Sky Mall. Grail translation of the Psalms.

"You will be heard," said Hildegard of Bingen once
and forever to whomever will listen.

I'm listening, Hildegard, but *my soul*, just like the Psalm says,
refuses to be consoled.

Everyone who got on board looked suspicious
or suspiciously like someone else.

Even me, even you.

Now the pilot has turned on the *fasten seat belt* sign
Now I'm getting ready for my debut:

Ladies and Gentlemen,
with my harp I will solve my problems.

THIS IS NOT AN ENTRANCE

In the box called June 17th, 1440 minutes in which to retreat or advance.

—

"Whenever that's happening, you have to ask yourself
if you're being brainwashed," a colleague said too loudly.

—

My husband dislikes my sour face, I've been informed,
but likes several of my others, thank goodness.

—

During sharing time, we clapped less during "Feliz Navidad"
in summer than when the children experimented
with balsa wood and you-just-never-know destruction.

—

If only all wishes came true so easily, I had said earlier, dreamy.

—

In real life, I hold up one hand to show my city.
On the map, Michigan leaned a little drunk. Tipsy mitten.

—

"Just then" the storm we'd only heard about on TV.

—

Shortly thereafter, I opened my mouth to decide—

Tie It to a Rock; Throw It in the River

Listening for the sound of arrival,
except I don't own that anymore.

That's ok; I'm not trying to get ahead.

Turns out the book that will change my life
already happened; I dusted myself off.

Which means I've just got to make it
a good habit of my own volition.

O to be a hostess! O to have a purpose!

And reader, I'm keeping you in mind.
Next time I run an errand, you come too—

Tuesday Progress Report

Another baby migraine
like a well-phrased question.

Feeling is active, I now realize.
Meaning lags behind, like thunder.

I could accomplish one of several items on my list.
I could tell you about dolls in trees, Mexico City,
ordinary sleeplessness.

I'm learning my limits: edge of town—

The note said, "This is the path to frustration."
The context has been forgotten.

Intuition tells me I'm fine.

I've not exceeded the day's maximum
dose of anything.
A song I like repeats in my mind.

Untitled or Not Yet

In order to make space for the sound . . .

A little brilliance here and a little something else . . .

Like churches and marriage . . .

The history of the arch is the history of *put your mind to it.*

You said, "she needs to slow down." But what was the context?
Getting more for your money? Check here for *maybe*?

I'm looking for a softening agent, God.
I'm looking to stand very still.

There's a lot of the fugitive in theory. Fuck that.

Now I'm only a little embarrassed, vaguely heartily sorry.

The erotic is not a mystery.
The keystone only seems to bear the most weight.
Innovation comes to those who want and know it.

What Have We Here

Then something sticky at the secret bottom
where my put hand stayed
strangely put.

Meanwhile, the face floated
considerably elsewhere
creasing and re-creasing its four corners:
eye and eye, mouth to mouth.

Thus, I was made.

Now,
one hand waves a wave you like,
one hand holds down the fort.

What You Won't Believe

Interruption #1: helicopter chop.
Interruption #2: so-so birdsong.

You choose.

Dewy perfection got me down. Last throes of childhood. Someone
rang a bell.

—I conceded.

Always thinking: I took too long.
Also: who will call my name?

Little owl, appliqué: this is the shape of a day.

Nobody wants to watch nothing happening, a student told me.

Too true; power grid.

I took my life—ratcheted it down for general consumption.

When You Reach an Obstacle

Two calm thoughts in a row. Personal best.

And I owe it all to grapefruit with powdered sugar:
private remedy, going on one week.

I had longed for something straightforward
and found it—*ta da!*—in the form of our friend citrus.

No scurvy for me.

No faux-smarts either, thanks.
That stuff is so exhausting.

A lot of people will be headed to the emergency room
given this summer's most popular sandals: itty bitty heel.

Can't wear that metaphor, can't read whatever's written
on the wall of the poetry I can't write.

I'm a sensible nonsensical girl, not the other way around.

Mostly, I defer to you.

In a fit of wisdom, you chose me.
What more can I say?

Who Are the New Saints and What Are Their Miracles

In the middle of the extremely on-time experience, I kept feeling late. Did someone say "paradox"? Did someone mean "wallowing"? Did anyone hear me chirp in the museum? One guard looked over; one looked sad. *Situation in Yellow*: my cheek coveting your hand. At the miniature village, this sign: "Be prepared to see more than you expect." *Is that possible?*, I whispered, cupping your fingers to my mouth. Or just imagining that as the freight elevator shook us up.

Wish and What Happens

—Back to the fe fi ho hum of it. *Don't flatter yourself*,
I told everyone else in my row on the plane. Or,
kind of did. Nothing could be more delightful
or more fearsome than the good rage I'm doing privately.
Do you consider yourself marked for luck? If so,
stoke it. I went all the way that way. Someday
someone will come after us; you can bet on it.
Someday they'll say *she was to him a mighty holler*.

You Can Get Tea Towels Like That

Beauty breaks in everywhere.

Welcome to the wind-powered poem.

Like the ocean or the woodcut of the ocean.

I heard the hardest things and listened.

Syntax says, *you first*. Shimmer half-scolds.

I said, *I am loved*. Sometimes a correction happens.

Fear made it one full week. A human action.

I stopped making it worse than it was.

Notes

"A Girl Can Imagine, Can't She, a Girl Can Dream": Sources include *The How and Why Wonder Book of Electricity, How to Make Marionettes,* and *The Little Alphabet.*

"An Ambiguity": Some language from brochures for Hartwick Pines State Park, Michigan.

"I Darken It Besides": Eva Hesse.

"Content / Content": Laurel Caverns, Pennsylvania.

"Her Sun Was Blue, Her Tree Was Green, Her Line Was Very Straight": from one of the *Miffy* books by Dick Bruna.

"Make Them Howl or Breathe Fire": title from *Scribbles: A Really Giant Drawing and Coloring Book* by Taro Gomi.

"There's No Time Like the Present": "Memory's logo is the abyss, and that's no metaphor" can be found in Charles Wright's "Transparencies" from *The Wrong End of the Rainbow.*

"Suppose We Make That Assumption": "These trees were cut illegally": a sign along I-75, just north of Bay City, Michigan. Detmar Finke first asked the question about Emily Dickinson.

"I Took Myself to Task": *"Is this adulthood or just bad fate?"*: Kelly Moffett asked this question.

"You Can Get Tea Towels Like That": title from Laura Brady. The first line is from Emerson.

Acknowledgments

ABZ: "Buzz Buzz Buzz," "Her Sun Was Blue, Her Tree Was Green, Her Line Was Very Straight," and "Tell 'em Why You're Special"

Cannibal: "What You Won't Believe"

Center: "Loud and Clear"and "There's No Time Like the Present"

Co*lumbia Poetry Review:* "I Want You to Scream It" and "Untitled or Not Yet"

Controlled Burn: "Churned Up"

Court Green: "Tuesday Progress Report"

Denver Quarterly: "Cinder Box," "I Darken It Besides," and "Part Two: Mystery"

Electronic Poetry Review: "You Can Get Tea Towels Like That"

Elixir: "Everything Sounds Almost Right in Poems."

Field: "I Whispered *Oh* Into His Ear," "Riskier Still," and "THIS IS NOT AN ENTRANCE"

Flights: "Bank On It," "I Took Myself to Task," and "Prototype"

Green Mountains Review: "In a Dark Time Together" and "Some Churches"

The Journal: "That's the Jesus I Grew Up With" and "Tie It to a Rock; Throw It in the River"

Kestrel: "Opting for Natalie Wood over Poetry"

Laurel Review: "An Introduction to Devotion," "Who Are the New Saints and What Are Their Miracles," and "Wish and What Happens"

Lyric Poetry Review: "*Content / Content*"

Meridian: "An Ambiguity" and "Make Them Howl or Breathe Fire."

Mid-American Review: "Introducing the Bird-watcher to the Bird," "Nail," "Ply Me with Something, Please," and "Smack-dab"

Night Sun: "Something Must Be Left to the Mystery"and "When You Reach an Obstacle"

Pank: "Quarterly Report"

Quarterly West: "Clarity, 1.2"

Third Coast: "In the Countryside of *The*"

Zone 3: "A Girl Can Imagine, Can't She, A Girl Can Dream," "From *The Little Book of Female Mystics*," "Incredibly Small and Impossibly Lovely," and "What Have We Here"

Thanks to my students and colleagues at West Virginia University, especially Gail Galloway Adams, Dennis Allen, Mark Brazaitis, and John Ernest; to friends and students at the Controlled Burn Seminar for Young Writers and the Far Field Retreat for Writers; to Bill Olsen; to Carol Finke, Brenda Hillman, Cindy Hite, Elissa Hoffman, Austin Hummell, Kelly Moffett, and Rebecca Emlinger Roberts; to Alex; to Ellen and Laura; and to my father.

Special thanks to Gerry: for poems that amaze and inspire, for love that sustains.

photo by Joy Gaines-Friedler

Mary Ann Samyn is the author of four books of poetry, most recently *Purr* (New Issues, 2005). Her work has won the Emily Dickinson Prize from the Poetry Society of America, the James Wright Poetry Award from *Mid-American Review,* and a Pushcart Prize. She teaches in the MFA program at West Virginia University.

New Issues Poetry

Vito Aiuto, *Self-Portrait as Jerry Quarry*
James Armstrong, *Monument in a Summer Hat*
Claire Bateman, *Clumsy, Leap*
Sandra Beasley, *Theories of Falling*
Kevin Boyle, *A Home for Wayward Girls*
Jason Bredle, *Standing in Line for the Beast*
Jericho Brown, *Please*
Michael Burkard, *Pennsylvania Collection Agency*
Christopher Bursk, *Ovid at Fifteen*
Anthony Butts, *Fifth Season; Little Low Heaven*
Kevin Cantwell, *Something Black in the Green Part of Your Eye*
Gladys Cardiff, *A Bare Unpainted Table*
Stacie Cassarino, *Zero at the Bone*
Kevin Clark, *In the Evening of No Warning*
Cynie Cory, *American Girl*
Peter Covino, *Cut Off the Ears of Winter*
James D'Agostino, *Nude with Anything*
Jim Daniels, *Night with Drive-By Shooting Stars*
Joseph Featherstone, *Brace's Cove*
Lisa Fishman, *The Deep Heart's Core Is a Suitcase*
Linda Nemec Foster, *Talking Diamonds*
Noah Eli Gordon, *A Fiddle Pulled from the Throat of a Sparrow*
Robert Grunst, *The Smallest Bird in North America*
Paul Guest, *The Resurrection of the Body and the Ruin of the World*
Robert Haight, *Emergences and Spinner Falls*
Mark Halperin, *Time as Distance*
Myronn Hardy, *Approaching the Center; The Headless Saints*
Brian Henry, *Graft*
Edward Haworth Hoeppner, *Rain Through High Windows*
Cynthia Hogue, *Flux*
Joan Houlihan, *The Mending Worm*
Christine Hume, *Alaskaphrenia*
Mark Irwin, *Tall If*
Josie Kearns, *New Numbers*
Claudia Keelan, *Missing Her*
David Keplinger, *The Clearing; The Prayers of Others*
Maurice Kilwein Guevara, *Autobiography of So-and-So: Poems in Prose*

Ruth Ellen Kocher, *When the Moon Knows You're Wandering; One Girl Babylon*
Gerry LaFemina, *The Window Facing Winter*
Steve Langan, *Freezing*
Lance Larsen, *Erasable Walls*
David Dodd Lee, *Abrupt Rural; Downsides of Fish Culture*
M.L. Liebler, *The Moon a Box*
Alexander Long, *Vigil*
Deanne Lundin, *The Ginseng Hunter's Notebook*
Barbara Maloutas, *In a Combination of Practices*
Joy Manesiotis, *They Sing to Her Bones*
Sarah Mangold, *Household Mechanics*
Gail Martin, *The Hourglass Heart*
Justin Marks, *A Million in Prizes*
David Marlatt, *A Hog Slaughtering Woman*
Louise Mathias, *Lark Apprentice*
Gretchen Mattox, *Buddha Box, Goodnight Architecture*
Carrie McGath, *Small Murders*
Paula McLain, *Less of Her; Stumble, Gorgeous*
Lydia Melvin, *South of Here*
Sarah Messer, *Bandit Letters*
Wayne Miller, *Only the Senses Sleep*
Malena Mörling, *Ocean Avenue*
Julie Moulds, *The Woman with a Cubed Head*
Carsten René Nielsen, *The World Cut Out with Crooked Scissors*
Marsha de la O, *Black Hope*
C. Mikal Oness, *Water Becomes Bone*
Bradley Paul, *The Obvious*
Jennifer Perrine, *The Body Is No Machine*
Katie Peterson, *This One Tree*
Jon Pineda, *The Translator's Diary*
Donald Platt, *Dirt Angles*
Elizabeth Powell, *The Republic of Self*
Margaret Rabb, *Granite Dives*
Rebecca Reynolds, *Daughter of the Hangnail; The Bovine Two-Step*
Martha Rhodes, *Perfect Disappearance*
Beth Roberts, *Brief Moral History in Blue*
John Rybicki, *Traveling at High Speeds* (expanded second edition)
Mary Ann Samyn, *Inside the Yellow Dress; Purr; Beauty Breaks In*
Ever Saskya, *The Porch is a Journey Different From the House*
Mark Scott, *Tactile Values*
Hugh Seidman, *Somebody Stand Up and Sing*
Heather Sellers, *The Boys I Borrow*
Martha Serpas, *Côte Blanche*

Diane Seuss-Brakeman, *It Blows You Hollow*
Elaine Sexton, *Sleuth; Causeway*
Patty Seyburn, *Hilarity*
Marc Sheehan, *Greatest Hits*
Heidi Lynn Staples, *Guess Can Gallop*
Phillip Sterling, *Mutual Shores*
Angela Sorby, *Distance Learning*
Matthew Thorburn, *Subject to Change*
Russell Thorburn, *Approximate Desire*
Rodney Torreson, *A Breathable Light*
Lee Upton, *Undid in the Land of Undone*
Robert VanderMolen, *Breath*
Martin Walls, *Small Human Detail in Care of National Trust*
Patricia Jabbeh Wesley, *Before the Palm Could Bloom: Poems of Africa*